PRAYERS

■ FOR ■

EXPECTANT PARENTS

LITURGY
TRAINING
PUBLICATIONS

ACKNOWLEDGMENTS

We are grateful to the many publishers and authors who have given permission to include their work. Every effort has been made to determine the ownership of all texts and to make proper arrangements for their use. We will gladly correct in future editions any oversight or error that is brought to our attention.

Unless otherwise noted, excerpts from scripture are from the *New American Bible with Revised New Testament and Psalms,* copyright © 1991, 1986, 1970 Confraterniy of Christian Doctrine, Inc., Washington, D.C. Used with permission. All rights reserved. No portion of the *New American Bible* may be reprinted without permission in writing from the copyright holder.

Excerpts from scripture on pp. 3, 9, 16, 18, 24, 30, 32, 34, and 48 are from the *New Revised Standard Version Bible* © 1989, Division of Christian Education of the National Council of the Churches of Christ in the United States of America. Used by permission. All rights reserved.

Acknowledgments continued on page 56.

PRAYERS FOR EXPECTANT PARENTS copyright © 2003 Archdiocese of Chicago: Liturgy Training Publications, 1800 North Hermitage Avenue, Chicago IL 60622-1101; 1-800-933-1800, fax 1-800-933-7094, e-mail orders@ltp.org. All rights reserved. See our website at www.ltp.org.

This book was compiled by Mary Caswell Walsh and edited by Lorie Simmons with assistance from Margaret Brennan and Laura Goodman. Carol Mycio was the production editor. The design is by Kari Nicholls, and the typesetting was done by her in Galliard, Jessamine, and Trajan fonts. The cover art © Collier Campbell Lifeworks/CORBIS. Interior art © 2003 www.ArtToday.com.

Printed in the United States of America.

Library of Congress Control Number: 2003109061

1-56854-462-6

PEXP

CONTENTS

FOREWORD

The time in which we await the birth of our child is a time of prayer. As we draw on the great reservoirs of God's love and strength in our desire to be good parents, not only is the child growing. We also grow.

"Prayer is waiting," said a Carmelite friend, describing his contemplative vocation. Pregnancy taught me what he meant. Jesus tells his disciples that to welcome a child is to welcome him. As we await the birth of our child, we are also welcoming Christ into our lives in new, wonderful, and life-altering ways.

I was in the last trimester of pregnancy with each of my children during Advent. My awareness of the kicking, squirming life within me became a meditation on our Advent expectations. I watched my body stretch and bulge and thought of "creation groaning" in travail, awaiting the children of light. Maranatha! How long, oh Lord?

My child was as near to me as my own heartbeat and yet a mystery. I wanted to meet this little person. As I pondered the awesome mystery unfolding, I became fascinated with all children; I searched the faces of strangers for a glimpse of my own child.

In the same way I ponder the mystery of Christ. He is as near to me as my heartbeat, yet unbearably distant. Impatient, I seek his face in the faces of others. Maranatha! Come quickly Lord, I long to see your face.

When birth pains began I embraced them gladly, knowing they would bring my child. When, at last, we held the baby, we counted and kissed each finger, each toe. Exhausted with the work and wonder of life, we gave heartfelt thanks. So may the joy of resurrection dwarf our fears of suffering. May the trials of family life give birth to thanksgiving.

Maranatha! Come quickly, Lord. You are ever welcome in our hearts and homes.

— *Mary Caswell Walsh*

You knit me in
my mother's womb.

PRAYERS FOR THE FIRST TRIMESTER

Morning Prayer

I love the LORD, who listened
    to my voice in supplication,
Who turned an ear to me
    on the day I called.

Gracious is the LORD and just;
    yes, our God is merciful.

    —Psalm 116:1–2, 5

God blessed them, and God said to them,
"Be fruitful and multiply, and fill the earth and
subdue it; and have dominion over the fish of
the sea and over the birds of the air and over
every living thing that moves upon the earth."

    —Genesis 1:28

INTERCESSIONS:

With an open heart, I pray:

✦ **Lord, send your hope and trust.**

For all expectant parents: ✦ *For those who wish to be parents:* ✦ *For children who need parents:* ✦ *For those struggling with an unexpected pregnancy:* ✦ [I pray also for . . .] ✦

May God, who chose to make known
    and to send
the blessings of eternal salvation
through the motherhood of the
    Blessed Virgin Mary
and the protection of Saint Joseph,
bless us and keep us in his care,
now and for ever.

    —*Catholic Household Blessings and Prayers*

Prayers for Evening

You formed my inmost being;
    you knit me in my mother's womb.
I praise you, so wonderfully you made me;
    wonderful are your works!
My very self you knew;
    my bones were not hidden from you,
When I was being made in secret,
    fashioned as in the depths of the earth.
Your eyes foresaw my actions;
    in your book all are written down;
    my days were shaped, before one came to be.

—*Psalm 139:13–16*

And Mary said,
    "My soul magnifies the Lord,
    and my spirit rejoices in God my Savior,
    for he has looked with favor on the
        lowliness of his servant.
    Surely, from now on all generations will call
        me blessed;

for the Mighty One has done great things
    for me,
and holy is his name.
His mercy is for those who fear him
from generation to generation.
He has shown strength with his arm;
he has scattered the proud in the thoughts
    of their hearts.
He has brought down the powerful from
    their thrones,
and lifted up the lowly;
he has filled the hungry with good things,
and sent the rich away empty.
He has helped his servant Israel,
in remembrance of his mercy,
according to the promise he made to our
    ancestors,
to Abraham and to his descendants forever."

—*Luke 1:46–55*

INTERCESSIONS:

With confidence in our all-seeing God, I pray:

✦ **Lord, let us feel the peace of your presence.**

For children afraid of the dark: ✦ *For aging parents:* ✦ *For busy, weary families:* ✦ *For those struggling with discomforts:* ✦ [I pray also for . . .] ✦

May God, the source of all patience and
     encouragement,
enable us to live in perfect harmony with
     one another
according to the spirit of Christ Jesus.

—*Catholic Household Blessings and Prayers*

Praise, Petition, and Reflection Through the Weeks

Creator of all life,
thank you for this precious gift.
The miracle of new life grows within me.
My heart leaps with joy and praise.
My mind trembles with awe and fear.

As this child grows within me,
help me to let go of the illusion of control
I once had over my body.
Help me to accept all the changes that
      are occurring.
Give to me a peaceful heart.
Help me to trust in all that is to come.
Be with me now.
My motherhood has already begun.

—*Kathryn A. Schneider*

Lord, I still can't believe
that I am going to be a father,
that a new life is going to come
into the world
because of me.

I don't think I'm ready
for what this all means,
for the changes between us,
for this new responsibility.

Prepare me, Lord, for what is to come.
Help me support my wife
during her pregnancy.
Help me to be aware
of what she is going through.
Give me patience when I feel forgotten.
Give me courage to face so many challenges.

Thank you, God, for the gift of our child.
Let me treasure this gift.
Help me to care for him well,
to be a good father,
a good role model,
and a good husband.

—*Robert M. Hamma*

Suddenly, you are. In an instant,
a fraction of a nanosecond; somewhere
between was not and is,
the not yet and now—you become.

Unaware of your presence; yet you are there.
Silently, without detection,
you come into being and take your place.

You change me; rearrange me,
without request.
You mold me into what you need;
my entire being complies.

A part of me, yet your own.
Miraculous metamorphosis within my womb;
that chrysalis of life.

Lost in wonder.
Both blessing and burden are mine,
as a piece of eternity
lodges deep within my members.
Part of an eternal plan set in motion.
And I, the chosen vessel, stand in awe;
blessed,
humbled,
undone.

—*Jill Noblit MacGregor*

Even before you had a name, we began
mothering and fathering the future.

—*Joel Solonche*

In those days Mary set out and went with haste
to a Judean town in the hill country, where
she entered the house of Zechariah and greeted
Elizabeth. When Elizabeth heard Mary's
greeting, the child leaped in her womb. And
Elizabeth was filled with the Holy Spirit and
exclaimed with a loud cry, "Blessed are you
among women, and blessed is the fruit of your
womb. And why has this happened to me, that
the mother of my Lord comes to me? For as
soon as I heard the sound of your greeting, the
child in my womb leaped for joy. And blessed
is she who believed that there would be a fulfill-
ment of what was spoken to her by the Lord."

—*Luke 1:39–45*

Come, O Mary, come and live in this house.
Give to each of us all the necessary spiritual
graces just as you brought them to the house
of Zachariah. . . . Be a light and joy for us as
you were in the family of Nazareth. Increase
our faith, our hope and charity.

—*Ronda De Sola Chervin and Carla Conley*

The threefold terror of love; a fallen flare
Through the hollow of an ear;
Wings beating about the room;
The terror of all terrors that I bore
The Heavens in my womb.

Had I not found content among the shows
Every common woman knows,
Chimney corner, garden walk,
Or rocky cistern where we tread the clothes
And gather all the talk?

What is this flesh I purchased with my pains,
This fallen star my milk sustains,

This love that makes my heart's blood stop
Or strikes a sudden chill into my bones
And bids my hair stand up?

—*William Butler Yeats, twentieth century*

Almighty God, giver of life and love,
bless N. and N.
Grant them wisdom and devotion
in the ordering of their common life,
that each may be to the other
a strength in need,
a counselor in perplexity,
a comfort in sorrow,
and a companion in joy.
And so knit their wills together in your will
and their spirits in your Spirit,
that they may live together in love and peace
all the days of their life;
through Jesus Christ our Lord.

—*Book of Common Worship*

Lord, behold our family here assembled.
We thank you for this place in which we dwell,
for the love that unites us,
for the peace given us this day,
for the hope with which we expect the morrow;
For the health, the work, the food,
    and the bright skies
that make our lives delightful;
for our friends in all parts of the earth.

Give us courage and gaiety and the quiet mind.
Spare to us our friends, soften to us our enemies.
Bless us, if it may be,
    in all our innocent endeavors;
if it may not, give us the strength to endure
    that which is to come;
that we may be brave in peril,
constant in tribulation,
temperate in wrath and in all changes of fortune
and down to the gates of death,
loyal and loving to one another.

As the clay to the potter,
as the windmill to the wind,
as children of their parent,
we beseech of you this help and mercy
for Christ's sake.

—Robert Louis Stevenson, nineteenth century

Come my Way, my Truth, my Life:
Such a Way, as gives us breath:
Such a Truth, as ends all strife:
Such a Life, as killeth death.

Come, my Light, my Feast, my Strength:
Such a Light, as shows a feast:
Such a Feast, as mends in length:
Such a Strength, as makes his guest.

Come, my Joy, my Love, my Heart:
Such a Joy, as none can move:
Such a Love, as none can part:
Such a Heart, as joys in love.

—George Herbert, seventeenth century

Be present, Lord,
in this time for waiting.

PRAYERS FOR THE SECOND TRIMESTER

Prayers for Morning

O LORD, our Lord,
> how awesome is your name through all
> > the earth!
> You have set your majesty above the heavens!
Out of the mouths of babes and infants
> you have drawn a defense against your foes,
> to silence enemy and avenger.
When I see your heavens, the work of your
> > fingers,
> the moon and stars that you set in place—
What are humans that you are mindful of them,
> mere mortals that you care for them?
Yet you have made them little less than a god,
> crowned them with glory and honor.

O LORD, our Lord,
> how awesome is your name through all
> > the earth!

> *—Psalm 8: 2–6, 10*

People were bringing little children to him
in order that he might touch them; and the
disciples spoke sternly to them. But when Jesus
saw this, he was indignant and said to them,
"Let the little children come to me; do not
stop them; for it is to such as these that the
kingdom of God belongs. Truly I tell you,
whoever does not receive the kingdom of God
as a little child will never enter it." And he
took them up in his arms, laid his hands on
them, and blessed them.

—*Mark 10:13–16*

INTERCESSIONS:

Awed by God's life-giving Spirit, I pray:

✦ **Enliven and sustain us, O Lord.**

For parents beginning their day's work: ✦ *For all
who will care for children today:* ✦ *For health care
workers and counselors who work with expectant
parents:* ✦ *For all people trying to adjust to
change:* ✦ [I pray also for . . .] ✦

As you await your child's birth in faith,
partners in God's own love, may you already
cherish the child you have conceived.

—*Catholic Household Blessings and Prayers*

Prayers for Evening

How varied are your works, LORD!
    In wisdom you have wrought them all;
    the earth is full of your creatures.

When you send forth your breath, they
        are created,
    and you renew the face of the earth.

May the glory of the LORD endure forever;
    may the LORD be glad in these works!

I will sing to the LORD all my life;
    I will sing praise to my God while I live.

—*Psalm 104:24, 30–31, 33*

You clothed me with skin and flesh,
    and knit me together with bones and sinews.
You have granted me life and steadfast love,
    and your care has preserved my spirit.

—*Job 10:11–12*

INTERCESSIONS:

Trusting in God's care, I pray:

✦ **Protect and nurture your people, O Lord.**

For families struggling with difficulties: ✦
For couples working for deeper understanding: ✦
For those suffering from fragile self confidence: ✦
For expectant parents in violent places: ✦
[I pray also for . . .] ✦

May the Lord make us overflow with
    love for one another and for all.
May God strengthen our hearts.

—*Catholic Household Blessings and Prayers*

Praise, Petitions, and Reflections through the Weeks

I have never been so full—
it spills from my eyes, pushes out from my belly
day by day hour by hour, I am larger.
Though I can never catch that moment
of motion and expansion,
any more than I could witness
the first cells dividing,
or the hands of the great-grandfather clock
    moving,
the moon arcing across the sky,
or the peony bush starting from green stubs
in my backyard, then flourishing into June
with wild pink happiness.

—*Andrea Potos*

Be present, Lord, in this time for waiting,
this blessed time that makes for us a baby.
May this child be carried with love and
    tenderness,

with wonder for the way our lives are knit
    together,
with joy for the strange and wonderful ways
    of your world.

—*Gabe Huck*

Unless the LORD build the house,
    they labor in vain who build.
Unless the LORD guard the city,
    in vain does the guard keep watch.

—*Psalm 127:1*

My Lord and Redeemer,
    Inside me is a sanctuary where You abide.
Inside my womb You fashion our child and
define every feature. The thought of Your
work is more than I can comprehend, and yet,
I delight in knowing that You are here. . . .
    I ask for my baby that its heart will be per-
fect. Four flawless chambers beating in perfect
sync. From there I envision the rest of the body

that has just begun: spinal cord, lungs, and brain. Oh Lord, our Creator, please complete each detail with precision and strength.

As the face and limbs begin to form, please grow sturdy bones and sound muscles. Make her eyes much stronger than mine. Give this dear little one ears that will hear for a lifetime. Give her a strong mind that will serve as an oasis for truth and wisdom. Lord, please oversee my baby's growth. Give our child legs to run and arms to hug. Fashion hands that are skillful, yet loving. I trust You to provide all that is needed.

Remember my baby until she's complete. Keep her safe inside until her time is appointed. I have faith because You are the maker of all, You stretched out the heavens, and spread out the earth. Your presence gives me peace. I will wait patiently while You work.

—*Angela Thomas Guffey*

The waiting of pregnancy is like the waiting we do for God. We carry hidden within ourselves new life. Not simply in the sense of renewal, but new life particularized, personalized, and uniquely enfleshed. We wait with unimaginable longing to see the face of the one we know to be already with us. Like an unborn child, the life of God grows unseen yet profoundly felt. Insistently pushing and prodding us, enlarging the contours of our lives and our hearts, as intimate to us as our own breathing, yet utterly other, the divine presence waits to be born.

—*Wendy M. Wright*

Creation awaits with eager expectation the revelation of the children of God; for creation was made subject to futility, not of its own accord but because of the one who subjected it, in hope that creation itself would be set free from slavery to corruption and share in the glorious freedom of the children of God. We know that all creation is groaning in labor

pains even until now; and not only that, but we
ourselves, who have the firstfruits of the Spirit,
we also groan within ourselves as we wait for
adoption, the redemption of our bodies. For
in hope we were saved. Now hope that sees for
itself is not hope. For who hopes for what one
sees? But if we hope for what we do not see,
we wait with endurance.

    —Romans 8:19—25

Dear God,
There are no words for the depth of my love
        for this child.
I pray for her and her protection.
I surrender her into Your hands.
Please, dear God, send Your angels to bless
        and surround her always.
May she be protected from the darkness
        of our times.
May she always see You at the center of her life.
May her heart grow strong,
To love You and serve You.

    —Marianne Williamson

The righteous walk in integrity—
    happy are the children who follow them!

    —*Proverbs 20:7*

Happy are all who fear the LORD,
    who walk in the ways of God.
What your hands provide you will enjoy;
    you will be happy and prosper.
Like a fruitful vine
    your wife within your home,
Like olive plants
    your children around your table.
Just so will they be blessed
    who fear the LORD.

    —*Psalm 128:1–4*

You are always with us, Lord,
You are water in the desert,
the fruit of life in the garden,
light at evening time.
In that way you are with us, Lord.

You are always with us, Lord,
You are the face reflected in the mirror,
the wine of joy at the celebration meal,
the sharing between friends.
In that way you are with us, Lord.

You are always with us, Lord.
You are the pilot in the boat,
the healer of the injured,
the parent in the home.
In that way you are with us, Lord.

—*Father Pierre-Etienne*

All that I am
sings of the God
who brings his life
to birth in me.
My spirit soars
on the wings of my Lord.
He has smiled on me
and the blaze of his smile
no woman or man
shall ever forget.

My God is a gentle strength
who has caught me up
and carried me to greatness.
His love
space cannot hold
nor time age
and all quicken to his touch.

My God is a torrent of justice.
He takes the straight paths
in the minds of the proud
and twists them to labyrinth.

The boot of the oppressor
he pushes aside
and raises the lowly,
whom he loves,
from the ground.

With his own hands
he sets a table for the hungry
but the unfeeling rich
suffer the cold eye
of his judgment.

Our mothers and our fathers
he has held in his arms
and the future grows
like this child within me
for the God of whom I sing
bears us his son.

—*John Shea*

ou drew me
forth from the womb.

PRAYERS FOR THE THIRD TRIMESTER

Prayers for Morning

The LORD is trustworthy in every word,
 and faithful in every work.
The LORD supports all who are falling
 and raises up all who are bowed down.
The eyes of all look hopefully to you;
 you give them their food in due season.
You open wide your hand
 and satisfy the desire of every living thing.
You, LORD, are just in all your ways,
 faithful in all your works.
You, LORD, are near to those who call upon you,
 to all who call upon you in truth.

My mouth will speak your praises, LORD;
 all flesh will bless your holy name forever.

 —*Psalm 145:13b–18, 21*

Joseph also went from the town of Nazareth in Galilee to Judea, to the city of David called Bethlehem, because he was descended from the house and family of David. He went to be registered with Mary, to whom he was engaged and who was expecting a child. While they were there, the time came for her to deliver her child. And she gave birth to her firstborn son and wrapped him in bands of cloth, and laid him in a manger, because there was no place for them in the inn.

—*Luke 2:4–7*

INTERCESSIONS:

With a longing heart, I pray:

✦ **Maranatha! Come, Lord!**

For those who are weary with waiting: ✦ *For those with inadequate health care:* ✦ *For parents unable to provide for their families:* ✦ *For creatures and creation awaiting new life:* ✦ [I pray also for . . .] ✦

Source of all blessings, Protector of infants,
look with favor on this child.

—*Catholic Household Blessings and Prayers*

Prayers for Evening

LORD, my heart is not proud;
    nor are my eyes haughty.
I do not busy myself with great matters,
    with things too sublime for me.
Rather, I have stilled my soul,
    hushed it like a weaned child.
Like a weaned child on its mother's lap,
    so is my soul within me.
Israel, hope in the LORD,
    now and forever.

—*Psalm 131*

Hannah said, "For this child I prayed; and the LORD has granted me the petition that I made to him. Therefore I have lent him to the LORD; as long as he lives, he is given to the LORD."

She left Samuel there for the LORD.

—*1 Samuel 1:27–28*

INTERCESSIONS:

With a keen sense of responsibility, I pray:

✦ **Lord, send your wisdom.**

For all those expecting their first child: ✦ *For children anticipating a new sibling: For all the extended family expecting a child:* ✦ *For health care workers serving newborns:* ✦ [I pray also for . . .] ✦

May the God of hope fill us with all joy and peace in believing so that by the power of the Holy Spirit + we may abound in hope.

—*William G. Storey*

Praise, Petition,
and Reflection through the Weeks

Lord God,
  Thank you for the life that kicks and squirms
                    inside me;
        my body that groans and creaks,
      but makes it through another day;
  a husband who does the dishes and overlooks
                    the mess;
  children who can't wait to see their new sibling;
            my church that prays;
          a friend who calls and listens;
      my parents who worry about their baby;
        my doctor and my insurance;
    little baby clothes sewn by faithful hands;
                Sunday naps;
  the freedom to abstain from new obligations;
  the sweet sense of anticipation that enhances
                  every day;
  our home, ready to be shared with another;
        your abundant provision for us;
  Preparing me to love another with my life;

your Son, the giver of eternal life, and the
model of grace.
In the name of the One Who came as a
baby, I praise You for blessings.

—*Angela Thomas Guffey*

Before she was in labor
  she gave birth;
before her pain came upon her
  she delivered a son.
Who has heard of such a thing?
  Who has seen such things?
Shall a land be born in one day?
  Shall a nation be delivered in one moment?
Yet as soon as Zion was in labor
  she delivered her children.
Shall I open the womb and not deliver?
  says the LORD;
shall I, the one who delivers, shut the womb?
  says your God.

Rejoice with Jerusalem, and be glad for her,
    all you who love her;
rejoice with her in joy,
    all you who mourn over her—
that you may nurse and be satisfied
    from her consoling breast;
that you may drink deeply with delight
    from her glorious bosom.
As a mother comforts her child,
    so I will comfort you;
    you shall be comforted in Jerusalem.

    —*Isaiah 66:7–11, 13*

You drew me forth from the womb,
    made me safe at my mother's breast.

    —*Psalm 22:10*

Good Lord,
you have tenderly loved us,
and given us this home and good friends.

May we make a true home for this child
Where he/she will learn trust in us and in you.
(May his/her brothers and sisters rejoice in
        their own growing up
as they help to care for this child.)
We ask this through Christ our Lord.

—*Catholic Household Blessings and Prayers*

Four corners to her bed
Four angels at her head
Mark, Matthew, Luke and John;
God bless the bed that she lies on.
New moon, new moon, God bless me
God bless this house and family.

—*Irish blessing for a child's bed*

Almighty God, from whom we receive
        our life,
you have blessed us with the joy and care
        of children.
As we bring them up,
give us calm strength and patient wisdom,
that we may teach them to love
whatever is just and true and good,
following the example of our Savior Jesus Christ.

    —*Book of Common Worship*

I surrender, dear God, my parenthood to You.
Make me the parent You want me to be.
Show me how to love most patiently,
        to be there for her most fully,
To understand profoundly who she is and
        what she needs.
May this family be a blessing unto her now
        and forever.
May she learn here values and principles of love
        and righteousness.
May she learn from me kindness.

May she learn from me strength.
May she learn from me the lessons of power:
That she has it and
Must surrender it to You, to be used for Your
purposes throughout her life
For thus shall You be gladdened,
And thus shall she be free,
To live most fully and love most deeply.
That is my wish.
That is my prayer for her and for me forever.

—*Marianne Williamson*

Lord, your love for us is like that of a mother
and you know the hard joy of giving birth.
Hold the hand of your servant now, keep
her safe;
put your own spirit into her very breathing
and into the nostrils of the new baby whom we
await with awe and hope.

—*Gabe Huck*

As Anne gave birth to Mary,
as Mary gave birth to Christ,
as Elizabeth gave birth to John the Baptist
without damage to foot or hand,
help this woman, O Son,
help her, help her, O Mother,
since it was you gave birth to the Son,
give bone to the unborn child
and keep the woman in safety.

   —*Irish prayer*

Lord God,
Receive with kindness the prayer of
      your servant
as she asks for the birth of a healthy child.
Grant that she may safely deliver a son
      or a daughter
to be numbered among your family,
to serve you in all things,
and to gain eternal life.

We ask this through Christ our Lord.

   —*Book of Blessings*

It's not for us to know if Mary's pain
Was dark or light, or how the labor went,
Or whether Joseph's energies were spent
Evicting some reluctant beast to gain
A corner of a manger's rich terrain
For purposes obstetric. Was he sent
To beggar, when the need was evident,
The help of women skilled in their domain?
It's left to our imagining to square
The rigors of the manger with the crèche,
To hear the muffled cry, to mark the stretch
And push a birthing God might bring to bear.
The image of the crèche is sweet and light,

But, Lord, was there no blood and sweat
    that night?

—*Christopher FitzGerald*

I pray God
In the hour of my pain
For this our child
Born of our bone,
Fashioned of our flesh,
Yet—mystery of God—
An immortal soul.

That he might know
Sweetness and warming at his mother's breast;
That he might grow
Wise, kind, benevolent beneath his father's hand;
That he might live
Before God's face
To goodly age spent following righteous ways.

What more to ask of God
For this our child
Born of our bone,
Fashioned of our flesh,
Yet—mystery of God—
An immortal soul.

—*Miriam Sieber Lind*

Under your
wings let me shelter
until faith and
courage return.

PRAYERS FOR ANXIOUS MOMENTS

O Lord, we beseech thee to deliver us from the fear of the unknown future; from fear of failure; from fear of poverty; from fear of bereavement; from fear of loneliness; from fear of sickness and pain; from fear of age; and from fear of death. Help us, O Father, by thy grace to love and fear thee only, fill our hearts with cheerful courage and loving trust in thee; through our Lord and Master Jesus Christ.

—*Akanu Ibaim, Nigeria*

The LORD is my light and my salvation;
    whom do I fear?
The LORD is my life's refuge;
    of whom am I afraid?

—*Psalm 27:1*

O God,
our every blessing comes from you
and you welcome the simple prayers
of those who bless your name.
Grant that this mother may live
in reliance on your goodness and in
        thankfulness to you.
Give to her and to her child the joyful
        reassurance
that you are always near to protect them.
We ask this through Christ our Lord.

—*Book of Blessings*

In you, LORD, I take refuge;
    let me never be put to shame.
In your justice deliver me;
    incline your ear to me;
    make haste to rescue me!
Be my rock of refuge,
    a stronghold to save me.
You are my rock and my fortress;
    for your name's sake lead and guide me.

—*Psalm 31:2–4*

My God and God of my ancestors—
You are ever nigh to all who call on You in truth.
I pray to You for strength.
Grant that my child may be born sound
     in mind and body,
with a happy nature and a good soul.
Grant that my beloved mate and I may be
     privileged to raise our child
in health and happiness with a sense of
     reverence for You and all others.
Blessed are You, Oh Lord, who hears
     our prayers.

    —*On the Wings of Healing*

God, tender and strong,
    as the plover defends her young
    against their enemies,
so defend me
    against those anxieties and nameless fears
    which are my enemies.
Save me in the hour of trial,
    and deliver me from evil.

Under your wings
    let me shelter
until faith and courage return:
for your love's sake.

—*Bruce D. Prewer*

Gracious Father,
your Word, spoken in love,
        created the human family
and your Son, conceived in love,
        restored it to your friendship.

Hear the prayers of N. and N.,
who await the birth of their child.
Calm their fears when they are anxious.

Watch over and support these parents
and bring their child into this world
safely and in good health,
so that as members of your family
they may praise you and glorify you
through your Son, our Lord Jesus Christ,
now and for ever.

—*Catholic Household Blessings and Prayers*

Dear Jesus,
as a hen covers her chicks with her wings
to keep them safe,
protect us this dark night
under your golden wings.

> —*prayer from the region of Bangladesh,*
>   *Bhutan and Nepal*

Send your peace into my heart, O Lord, that I
may be contented with the mercies of this day
and confident of your protection this night;
and having forgiven others, even as you forgive
me, may I go to rest in tranquility and trust;
through Jesus Christ our Lord.

> —*Saint Francis of Assisi, thirteenth century*

God of all our days:
like a parent you forgive us,
and like a child you love us.
May we love and forgive one another.

> —*Catholic Household Blessings and Prayers*

Be still and know that I am God!

—*Psalm 46:10a*

Lord Jesus Christ, Good Shepherd of the sheep, you gather the lambs in your arms and carry them in your bosom: We commend to your loving care this child *N.* Relieve *his* pain, guard *him* from all danger, restore to *him* your gifts of gladness and strength, and raise *him* up to a life of service to you. Hear us, we pray, for your dear Name's sake.

—*The Book of Common Prayer*

God of love,
ever caring, ever strong,
stand by us in our time of need.

—*Catholic Household Blessings and Prayers*

Merciful God,
Enfold N. [*name of child*] in the arms
    of your love.
Comfort N., N. [*parent(s)*] in their anxiety.
Deliver *them* from despair,
give *them* patience to endure
and guide *them* to choose wisely for
    N. [*name of child*],
in the name of him who welcomed
    little children,
even Jesus Christ our Lord.

—*Book of Common Worship*

Where can I hide from your spirit?
    From your presence, where can I flee?
If I ascend to the heavens, you are there;
    if I lie down in Sheol, you are there too.
If I fly with the wings of dawn
    and alight beyond the sea,
Even there your hand will guide me,
    your right hand hold me fast.

—*Psalm 139:7–12*

What will separate us from the love of Christ?
Will anguish, or distress, or persecution, or
famine, or nakedness, or peril, or the sword?
No, in all these things we conquer over-
whelmingly through him who loved us. For
I am convinced that neither death, nor life,
nor angels, nor principalities, nor present
things, nor future things, nor powers, nor
height, nor depth, nor any other creature will
be able to separate us from the love of God
in Christ Jesus our Lord.

—*Romans 8:35, 37–39*

May God, who is blessed above all,
bless us in all things through Christ,
so that whatever happens in our lives
will work together for our good.

—*Catholic Household Blessings and Prayers*

For the gift of this
child we give thanks.

Prayers of Thanksgiving

How dark was everything around me but
a few hours ago; anxiety filled my heart, and
I was afraid of the results of my fears and
pain. But when I called in my woe, the Lord
heard me, and saved me from my troubles.
The hours of anxiety have passed, and now
joy and light surrounded me. . . . I praise
Thy mercy, and shall never forget Thy benefits;
my heart and mouth shall ever overflow with
thanks and praises of Thy supreme power and
loving-kindness.

My God and Lord! Bestow Thy protection
upon my newborn infant, that it may thrive
and grow, and be healthful in body and soul.

—*Fanny Neuda*

O gracious God, we give you humble and
hearty thanks that you have preserved through
the pain and anxiety of childbirth your servant
N., who desires now to offer you her praises
and thanksgivings. Grant, most merciful Father,
that by your help she may live faithfully according to your will in this life, and finally partake
of everlasting glory in the life to come;
through Jesus Christ our Lord.

    —*The Book of Common Prayer*

My God and Helper—You have answered my
       prayer and have
blessed our world and my life with this child.
Accept my thankfulness for Your great loving
       kindness.
Give me the strength, the means and the
       insight to raise this child to be
loving and kind to all and ever loyal to You,
       and to all humankind.

    —*On the Wings of Healing*

Blessed is the Lord our God, Ruler of the universe, for giving us life, for sustaining us, and for enabling us to reach this happy day.

O God, for the gift of this child we give thanks, praying that we will be worthy of the blessing and responsibility of parenthood.

—Jewish blessing and thanksgiving for a new child

O God, you have taught us through your blessed Son that whoever receives a little child in the name of Christ receives Christ himself: We give you thanks for the blessing you have bestowed upon this family in giving them a child. Confirm their joy by a lively sense of your presence with them, and give them calm strength and patient wisdom as they seek to bring this child to love all that is true and noble, just and pure, lovable and gracious, excellent and admirable, following the example of our Lord and Savior, Jesus Christ.

—The Book of Common Prayer

Mighty God,
by your love we are given children
through the miracle of birth.
May we greet each new son and daughter
with joy,
and surround them all with faith,
so they may know who you are
and want to be your disciples.
Never let us neglect children,
but help us enjoy them,
showing them the welcome you have
shown us all;
through Jesus Christ the Lord.

—*Book of Common Worship*

Acknowledgments continued from page ii.

May God, p. 2: from the English translation of *Book of Blessings* © 1988, International Committee on English in the Liturgy, Inc. (ICEL). All rights reserved.

As you, p. 17; God of love, p. 48; and May God, p. 50: from the English translation of *Pastoral Care of the Sick* © 1982, International Committee on English in the Liturgy, Inc. (ICEL). All rights reserved.

May God, p. 5; May the Lord, p. 18; Source of all, p. 31; Good Lord, p. 36; Gracious Father, p. 46; and God of all, p. 47: from *Catholic Household Blessings and Prayers,* © 1988, United States Catholic Conference, Inc., Washington, D.C. Reprinted with permission. All rights reserved.

Creator of, p. 5–6; and Lord, I, p. 6: excerpted from *Let's Say Grace: Mealtime Prayers for Family Occasions Throughout the Year* by Robert M. Hamma. Copyright © 1995 by Ave Maria Press, P.O. Box 428, Notre Dame, IN 46556, www.avemariapress.com. Used with permission of the publisher.

Suddenly, you, p. 7–8; and I have, p. 19: excerpted from *Mothers and Daughters: A Poetry Celebration* compiled by June Cotner. New York: Harmony Books, © 2001 by June Cotner.

Even before, p. 9: "Acrostic for Our Daughter, June 1995" copyright Joel Solanche, from *Peach Girl: Poems for a Chinese Daughter,* Grayson Books, 2002.

Come, O, p. 10: from *The Book of Catholic Customs and Traditions* by Ronda De Sola Chervin and Carla Conley © 1994 by Ronda De Sola Chervin and Carla Conley. Published by Servant Publications, P.O. Box 8617, Ann Arbor, Michigan 48107. Used with permission.

The threefold, p. 10: reprinted with the permission of Scribner, an imprint of Simon and Schuster Adult Publishing Group, from *The Collected Works of W. B. Yeats, Volume I: The Poems, Revised* edited by Richard J. Finnaran. Copyright © 1933 by The Macmillan Company, copyright renewed © 1961 by Bertha Georgle Yeats. Permission also granted by A.P. Watt Ltd. on behalf of Michael B. Yeats.

Almighty God, p. 11; Lord, behold, p. 12; Almighty God, p. 37; Merciful God, p. 49; and Mighty God, p. 55: from *Book of Common Worship* ©

Westminster John Knox Press 1993. Used by permission of Westminster John Knox Press.

Come my, p. 13: from *George Herbert, The Country Parson, The Temple* ed. John N. Wall, Jr. Copyright © 1981, Paulist Press, Inc., New York/Mahwah, New Jersey. Used with permission of Paulist Press. www.paulistpress.com.

Be present, p. 19–20; and Lord, your, p. 38: from *A Book of Family Prayer* by Gabe Huck. New York: Seabury Press, 1979. Used with permission by the author.

My Lord, p. 20; and Lord God, p. 33–34: reprinted by permission of Thomas Nelson Inc., Nashville, TN, from the book entitled *Prayers for the Mother to Be* copyright date 2003 by Angela Thomas. All rights reserved.

The waiting, p. 22: from *The Vigil: Keeping Watch in the Season of Christ's Coming.* Copyright © 1992 by Wendy M. Wright. Used by permission of Upper Room Books.

Dear God, p. 23; and I surrender, p. 37–38: from Illuminata by Marianne Wilson, copyright © 1994 by Marianne Williamson. Used by permssion of Random House, Inc.

All that, p. 26: from *The God Who Fell from Heaven* copyright © by John Shea, published by The Thomas More Press, Chicago.

You are, p. 25: from *Extending the Table . . . A World Community Cookbook* by Joetta Handrich Schlabach and Kristina Mast Burnett, Herald Press, Scottdale, Pennsylvania 15683. All rights reserved.

May the, p. 32: from *An Everyday Book of Hours* by William G. Storey. Chicago: Liturgy Training Publications, 2001.

Four corners, p. 36: from *Irish Blessings, Toasts & Traditions* edited by Jason S. Roberts. New York: Barnes & Nobel Books, 1993. Copyright © 1993 Jason S. Roberts. Reprinted by kind permission of Mercier Press Ltd., Cork.

I pray, p. 41: from *Meditations for the Expectant Mother* by Helen Good Brenneman, Herald Press, Scottdale, Pennsylvania 15683. All rights reserved.

As Anne, p. 39: from *Saltair, Prayers from the Irish Tradition* by Padraig O Fiannachta, tr. Desmond Forristal. Dublin: The Columba Press, Copyright © 1988, Desmond Forristal.